Important events in the life of

Pieter Bruegel

1525	Pieter Bruegel is born around this time near Breda in present day Holland. The exact date of Bruegel's birth is unknown.
1551	Becomes a Master of the Painters' Guild in Antwerp.
1552	Travels to Italy and visits Reggio, Messina, Palermo and Naples.
1553	Meets Clovio in Rome.
1554	Spends time in Switzerland and makes drawings of the Alps.
1555	Returns to Antwerp and works for Hieronymus Cock, an engraver and publisher of prints.
1559	Begins to spell his name Bruegel instead of Brueghel.
1562	Spends more and more time painting.
1563	Marries in Brussels and settles there. His wife, Mayken, is the daughter of Pieter Coeck van der Aelst and Mayken Verhulst.
1564	Elder son Pieter is born.
1565	Paints a series of paintings called *The Months* for Niclaes Jonghelinck.
1568	Second son Jan is born.
1569	Bruegel dies and is buried in Notre Dame de la Chapelle, in Brussels.
1578	Mayken Bruegel dies.
1604	Carl van Mander includes a life of Bruegel in his book on the history of painting in northern Europe.

Daphne Butler

An introduction to Pieter Bruegel

Pieter Bruegel, artist unknown, 1572

HODDER Wayland

an imprint of Hodder Children's Books

Children's Games, 1560
Pictures in the 16th century were like television today – they aimed to amuse and inform people. In this painting, Bruegel shows 80 different games that were popular with children at that time. The children range from toddlers to teenagers and they occupy not only the square and the river area in the top left-hand corner, but also the large building at the back of the square. This could be the town hall.

Cover: The Peasant Wedding, 1567

End paper: detail from The Hunters in the Snow, 1565

Title page: Engraving from a Dutch manuscript

Paintings in this book are identified by their title followed by the artist who painted them. If no artist is named the painting is by Pieter Bruegel.

This book was prepared for Macdonald Young Books Ltd by Tucker Slingsby Creative Services 3G London House 66–68 Upper Richmond Road London SW15 2RP

Project Editor: Katie Preston
Editor: Jackie Fortey
Picture Researcher: Liz Eddison
Design concept by M&M Design Partnership
Designer: Steve Rowling
Artwork: George Fryer, Bernard Thornton Artists

Consultant: Tom Parsons

Subject Adviser
Professor Arthur Hughes
Department of Art, University of Central England, Birmingham

First published in Great Britain in 1996 by Macdonald Young Books Ltd
This edition published in 2001 by Hodder Wayland, an imprint of Hodder Children's Books

Printed by GRAFIASA S.A., Porto, Portugal

Acknowledgements
l = left; r = right; t = top; b = bottom

Bridgeman Art Library: Front Cover: Kunsthistorisches Museum, Vienna; Front End Paper: Kunsthistorisches Museum, Vienna; Kunsthistorisches Museum, Vienna 4, 9, 11, 17t, 18, 23, 24, 25; Prado Madrid 6l, 10, 14, 15t; Private collection 6r, 7t; Christie's London 7b, 12; National Gallery, London 8t, 21; Giraudon 8b; Musées Royaux des Beaux-Arts De Belgique 16; Narodni Galerie, Prague 17b; Gemaldegalerie, Kunsthistorisches Museum, Vienna 19; Museo E Gallerie Nazionali di Capodimonte, Naples 20; Johnny Van Haeften Gallery, London 26, 28; Hessisches Landesmuseum, Darmstadt 27; Galleria Dell'Accademia Carrara, Bergamo 29.

The British Museum 15b.

A catalogue record for this book is available from the British Library

ISBN 0 7502 3524 1

Contents

Troubled times

Nobody is sure when, or where, Pieter Bruegel was born. It may have been in 1525 near to a town called Breda, which is today in Holland. Then, Holland and Belgium were known as the Low Lands and were part of a vast, powerful empire controlled by the King of Spain. The Low Lands were the crossroads of Europe. Merchants came from all directions to exchange their goods, bringing new ideas and inventions from distant places.

Pieter Bruegel spent much of his life in Antwerp, a thriving port on the North Sea.

▲ Erasmus, Hans Holbein, 1523
Erasmus was a Dutch scholar and writer who put forward the view that people should progress through their own efforts rather than relying on the Church to look after them. At this time the Church was very powerful.

Change was in the air in Europe in the 1500s. Europeans had landed in America and discovered a whole new continent.

In Italy, artists were creating great works of art. In Germany, people were demanding to worship God in their own way. And, most important of all, a machine had been invented to print books.

◀ Charles V at the Battle of Muhlberg, Titian, 1548
In 1540s, there were religious riots. People wanted the Church to accept new ideas. Charles V of Spain put down the rebellion. The Italian painter, Titian, painted Charles riding into battle to commemorate this.

▼ The Low Lands
In Bruegel's time, the area we know today as Belgium and Holland was ruled by Spain. Bruegel lived in a part of Belgium near to the sea which is known as Flanders.

▲ Amsterdam in the 1500s, D G Hucquier
Amsterdam and Antwerp were both busy ports. In 1576 the people of Antwerp rose up against Spanish rule but were defeated. After this, Amsterdam became the main port.

Towns like Antwerp were becoming very rich. They imported food, cloth and dyes and exported furniture, tapestries, paintings, books, maps, musical instruments and many other goods.

Pieter Bruegel lived at the centre of this changing world and his paintings give us an idea of what life was like for ordinary people.

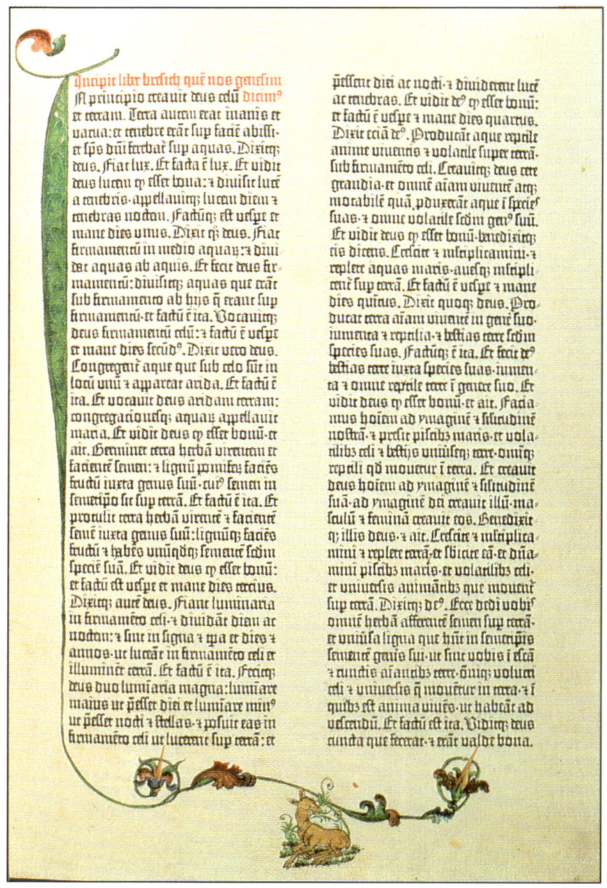

▲ The Gutenberg Bible, about 1450–55
When Johann Gutenberg invented a printing press, a Bible was one of the first books he printed. Within 50 years printing was an important trade across all Europe.

Flemish art

Flemish art describes the kind of pictures painted by artists who lived in Flanders from about 1400 to 1700. Flemish artists drew detailed pictures of the world in which they lived. Jan van Eyck is the most famous of the early Flemish painters. Rubens was the most important of the later ones. But the uncertain times of the 1500s have given us only one great master – Pieter Bruegel.

▲ Giovanni Arnolfini and his Wife, Jan van Eyck, 1434
This is one of Jan van Eyck's best works. It is a splendid double portrait, celebrating the marriage of an Italian merchant. Jan worked for the Duke of Burgundy as his official painter and manservant. In 1430, the Duke moved his household to Bruges, which became an important artistic centre.

▼ The Coronation of Marie de Medici, Peter Paul Rubens, 1621–25
Rubens was a very successful Flemish artist, and was known throughout Europe. He had a studio in Antwerp where many young artists came to learn. Pieter Bruegel's son, Jan, worked at Rubens' studio.

▲ **The Fight between Carnival and Lent, 1559**
The Flemish carnival was held every year just before Lent. It was a time of feasting and merry making. Lent was a time to fast for 40 days until Easter. The fight is the joust taking place at the front of the picture. The rest of the painting is crammed with interesting details and events.

Bruegel had a very different kind of life to van Eyck and Rubens, who had royal patrons. He did not work for royal households, or paint for churches, nor did he paint portraits of famous people. Bruegel was interested in the way ordinary people lived.

Bruegel's pictures are always fascinating. Everywhere you look something is happening. He painted strong outlines filled in with colour· which make very dramatic scenes, full of movement and detail.

■ *Bruegel has painted the scene from a high view-point: we see it as if we are looking down on it from above.*

Ways of painting

In the Middle Ages, European artists often painted on wooden panels. The panels were first coated with a mixture of chalk and glue. This was known as gesso and it made a smooth white surface on which to paint. Artists made their own paints by mixing coloured materials with egg yolk. The paint was known as egg tempera.

▲ Egg tempera
Before oil paints became popular, artists mixed powdered materials with egg yolk to make paint.

Some of the colours were made from crushed rock and others from parts of plants or animals. Egg tempera was not easy to use. There were not many colours and they were difficult to blend together. In the 1400s, artists started grinding their colours into oils such as linseed or walnut oil. This paint was much better. Today, oil paints are made in factories and sold in metal tubes so the paint can be squeezed out easily.

◀ The Empress Isabella of Portugal, Titian, 1548
Titian was a famous Italian artist. In this portrait, he used oil paints to get many different textures ranging from the smoothness of ice to the roughness of fabric. Other artists studied his work to get the same effects.

▲ **The Peasant and the Bird Nester, 1568**
This painting illustrates an old Flemish proverb: 'He who knows where the nest is, knows it; he who has the nest, has it.' This seems to mean that it is no use having knowledge if you do not act upon it.

In the 1400s and 1500s, Italy had many talented artists who painted beautiful pictures. The people in the paintings were usually shown as young and attractive. The scenery and buildings were always exquisite.

Artists travelled from all over Europe, visiting cities such as Rome, Florence and Venice, to learn painting skills from Italian masters like Titian.

■ *The massive limbs of the peasant striding towards us are one of the most striking things about this painting. Bruegel was inspired by the size and scale of figures painted by the Italian artist Michelangelo, which he had seen during a trip to Italy. At the same time, he painted the leaves of the trees with tiny, delicate brushstrokes.*

Foreign travel

The first we know of Bruegel is as a young man in Antwerp. Experts think he trained with Pieter Coeck van Aelst. Pieter Coeck was a well known artist who painted in the Italian style. He had studios in both Antwerp and Brussels. Pieter Coeck's wife Mayken was an expert worker in watercolour and egg tempera and may have taught Bruegel to paint with these.

In 1551, Bruegel became a Master of the Painters' Guild in Antwerp and a year later set off for Italy to learn more about Italian art and artists. We know that he visited Reggio, Messina, Palermo and Naples before travelling on to Rome.

In Rome he met Guilio Clovio who was an expert painter of very small pictures, known as miniatures. Bruegel did several paintings while staying with Clovio but these have been lost.

On his way home, Bruegel stayed for a while in Switzerland where the spectacular mountain scenery caught his imagination. By 1555, he was once more back in Antwerp.

◀ The Outskirts of Antwerp in Winter, Jan Brueghel and Joos de Momper
When Pieter Bruegel visited Italy he would have found the weather and the customs very different to those of his home town of Antwerp. This picture of Antwerp was painted some years later by his son and a friend. It shows a sturdy, prosperous town which was quite unlike the grand, sunny cities of Italy.

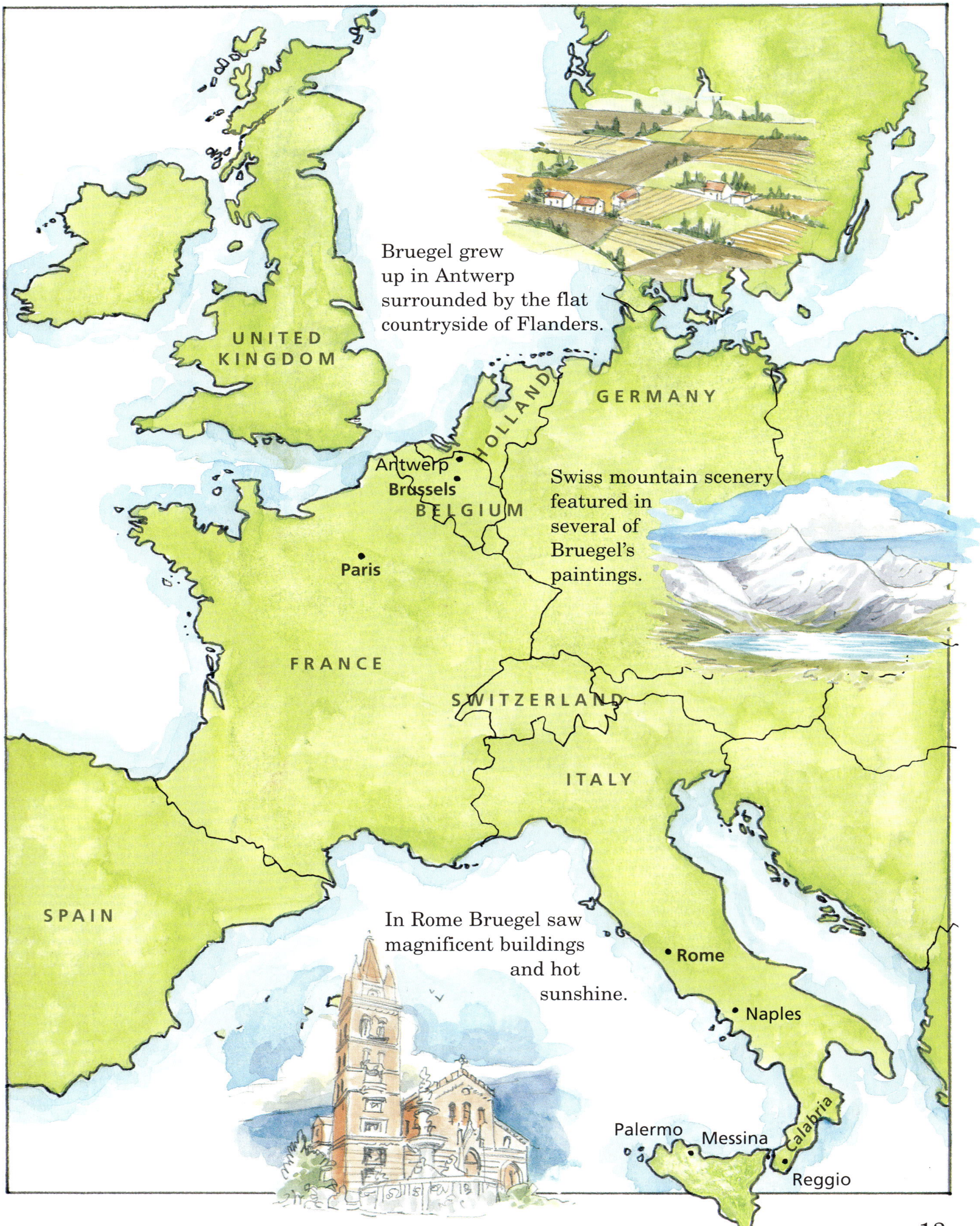
Bruegel grew up in Antwerp surrounded by the flat countryside of Flanders.
UNITED KINGDOM
HOLLAND
GERMANY
Antwerp
Brussels
BELGIUM
Paris
FRANCE
Swiss mountain scenery featured in several of Bruegel's paintings.
SWITZERLAND
ITALY
SPAIN
In Rome Bruegel saw magnificent buildings and hot sunshine.
Rome
Naples
Calabria
Palermo
Messina
Reggio

Designer and painter

On his return to Antwerp, Bruegel went to work for Hieronymus Cock, who was an engraver and print seller. Bruegel made drawings that the engravers could turn into prints. People were keen to learn about the world, but travel was difficult. Instead, they collected prints by artists like Bruegel, who had travelled abroad.

Prints of work by Hieronymus Bosch, a Flemish artist who lived in the late 1400s, were still very popular in the 1500s. Bosch's work was often full of demons and strange creatures. Cock set Bruegel to work making drawings in the same style. Bruegel worked for Cock all his life but, after 1562, spent more time on his own painting.

◀ **The Garden of Earthly Delights: Hell, Hieronymus Bosch, about 1500**
Bosch's work was very popular and was collected by Philip II of Spain. This is a detail of one part of an altar-piece. It shows the terrors of hell. The scene is like one from a nightmare, and it is full of meaning. It warns of what will happen to the sinful. It is easy to see the effect of this powerful style of painting on Bruegel's work.

▲ **Triumph of Death, 1562–63**
Part of a painting done by Bruegel in the style of Hieronymus Bosch. The frightening skeleton army means death for the living. No one, young or old, king or beggar, can escape its clutches.

▼ **Country Concerns, 1555**
This is an engraving made from one of Bruegel's landscape drawings. The engravings were made by craftsmen in the workshop of Hieronymus Cock.

■ *To make an engraving, a drawing is copied on to a copper plate using a sharp tool called a burin. The burin is pushed along the surface of the metal making a v-shaped groove. When the drawing is finished, the copper plate is covered in ink and used to print copies of the picture. So from one drawing many prints can be made.*

People and landscape

▲ **The Fall of Icarus, about 1555**
This is one of Bruegel's earliest surviving paintings. It tells a story, from Greek mythology, of a boy called Icarus who made wings out of feathers stuck together with wax. Icarus flew too close to the sun, the heat melted the wax and he fell into the sea. It also reflects the Flemish proverb: 'No plough stops because a man dies'. Look for Icarus' legs to the right of the picture.

It seems that, at first, Bruegel was only really interested in painting pictures of the countryside. He often added mountains, like those he had seen in Switzerland, to scenery that was typically Flemish. Later, he began to add figures, often borrowing ideas from Hieronymus Bosch and using them in his own way. His paintings became crammed with figures and groups of people.

Most of Bruegel's early paintings have been lost over the years. Of the 48 now known to exist, many were done towards the end of his life.

▶ **The Gloomy Day, 1565**
Bruegel has painted the dark stormy month of February, when peasants gather wood for their fires, repair their roofs and protect their stores from the winter weather.

■ *At about the time when they began to paint with oil rather than egg tempera, artists began to paint on canvas rather than wooden panels. Canvas was much quicker to prepare.*

▲ **Haymaking, 1565**
By 1565, Bruegel had left Bosch's style behind. There are fewer figures in his paintings and they are arranged in groups that blend in with the countryside. In this delightful landscape, Bruegel is showing how the lives of country people must follow the weather and the seasons.

The Months

In 1565, Bruegel was asked to paint a series of scenes for a wealthy Antwerp merchant called Niclaes Jonghelinck. The inside of his large house had been redecorated and the pictures were part of the scheme.

Six paintings are known about, but some experts believe there may even have been twelve – one for each month.

▲ **Merchant's house in Antwerp**

▼ **The Hunters in the Snow, 1565**
For this landscape of Flanders, Bruegel 'borrowed' the mountains from Switzerland and the figures trudging over the hill from Italian art. One of the reasons why Bruegel is such a great painter is because he could use different ideas to produce a picture that looks real.

▲ **The Return of the Herd, 1565**
Here, the cows are being driven down from the mountains to spend the winter in the village.

■ *Bruegel used a brown gesso, then drew the outlines with a thin brush. Afterwards he added the colour allowing the gesso to show through to give a warm brown glow. His figures, trees and distant buildings are shown by quick brushstrokes, with every line and patch of colour in its proper place.*

By the time he painted *The Months*, Bruegel had a sure, swift technique. He worked quickly with thin paint. Sometimes the gesso base became part of the painting. The series was completed by February 1566. The paintings showed the changing seasons. A whole year unfolded on the walls of a single room. It must have been a stunning sight.

Jonghelinck was a great admirer of Bruegel's work. By the time Bruegel died he owned 16 of his paintings.

The five Months that still exist are *Haymaking* (see page 17), *The Corn Harvest*, *The Return of the Herd* (above), *The Hunters in the Snow* (opposite) and *The Gloomy Day* (page 17).

Moral tales

Bruegel must have been very interested in people. His work often shows the funny, strange or foolish things that people do.

Sometimes Bruegel chose parables and stories from the Bible as the theme or story for his paintings. Sometimes he chose proverbs and moral sayings. Moral stories and proverbs were also popular subjects for amateur plays, which were performed in Bruegel's home town.

The story of blind men leading each other into a ditch was told by Jesus. Many artists have painted it, but Bruegel's painting is one of the best.

▼ **Parable of the Blind, 1568**
Bruegel's blind men stumble along, each one following the man in front. They are about to follow their leader, falling headlong into the ditch. The message is: 'Choose your leaders carefully.'

■ *The picture has a very strong design, with the figures moving in a diagonal line across it. We cannot help looking at the men and wondering where they will fall.*

▶ The Adoration of the Magi, 1564
This painting was an important turning point in Bruegel's work. For the first time he used a group of large figures and he painted the faces in great detail. The faces show how each person feels about the baby on the mother's lap.

■ *Bruegel has borrowed this composition from Italian art, but he is using it in a different way. He set out to make his figures seem full of character rather than beautiful, as was the Italian style of painting.*

Bruegel painted several stories from the New Testament, including the visit by the wise men or 'magi' to see the baby Jesus. The wise men brought expensive gifts with them, which they left with the child.

Bruegel painted other stories from the New Testament. These include Jesus on the way to Calvary where He was crucified and St Paul becoming a follower of Christianity after a vision on the road to Damascus.

The Tower of Babel

The Tower of Babel is an Old Testament story about the dangers of pride. Bruegel painted the scene three times. The first painting was a small picture on ivory which he left in Rome with Clovio and which no longer exists. The second is dated 1563 and is the one shown here. The third is a little smaller and was painted later.

The story takes place after the great flood. The people found a plain near the River Euphrates and built a city there which they called Babylon. The place where Babylon stood is in modern-day Iraq, in the Middle East.

The city was very successful and the people believed they could do whatever they liked.

They started to build a tower that reached high into the sky. God decided they were becoming too vain and self-important. He mixed up their language so they could no longer speak to each other. To add to the confusion, He made the tower crumble.

The picture has a strong moral message showing that 'pride comes before a fall'. The frantic efforts of the workmen trying to rebuild the huge structure was Bruegel's way of showing how little people can do against the will of God.

The people of the Low Lands belonged to an empire that was beginning to break up. They would have understood the message of this painting.

▶ Colosseum in Rome
This vast amphitheatre was started by Emperor Vespasian about AD 75 and completed by his sons. It could hold 50,000 people seated in three tiers with some standing above. The tiers were joined by staircases. The arena was used for contests between gladiators, fights between men and beasts and for mock battles. Bruegel based his painting of the Tower of Babel on the Colosseum.

▲ **The Tower of Babel, 1563**
Once again Bruegel has told an ancient story as though it was happening at the time he painted it. The houses in the city, the ships on the river and the clothes the people are wearing are all typical of Flanders in the 1500s. The workmen on the tower give an accurate picture of how buildings were constructed in Bruegel's day.

■ *Look closely at the detail from the picture to see the many kinds of building machines and workmen with different skills.*

■ *Bruegel must have been an expert on building techniques. Just before he died he was asked to make a series of paintings to record the building of a canal linking Brussels and Antwerp. These paintings were never finished.*

Peasant Bruegel

▲ **The Peasant Wedding, 1567**
In this picture you can see the bride has a central position under the canopy at the back of the table. The bridegroom may be the man in black who is leaning on his stool calling for more wine. When people get married they make serious promises, but Bruegel is showing how weddings become an excuse for a party. The richly dressed nobleman on the far right is perhaps the local landowner. He is talking to the monk who may have married the couple.

Bruegel painted peasant life many times. It is said that, with a friend, he disguised himself as a peasant and went to weddings and festivals. These two pictures may have been a pair of paintings or part of a series that Bruegel had planned. They are the two best examples of his later style, which featured large, solid figures. Like many of his pictures, they have a moral message to give us.

■ *Although Bruegel painted peasant subjects, peasants could not afford to buy his pictures. They were bought by rich merchants and educated people.*

Bruegel was an educated man and his friends were thinking people who cared about humanity. He was successful and well-respected in his lifetime. But after his death fashions changed and people lost interest in his work. His paintings were thought to be ugly and some of them must have been destroyed and so disappeared for ever.

▼ The Peasant Dance, 1567

A village celebration for a Saint's day is in full swing. The revellers have their backs to the church and are more interested in their own enjoyment than in remembering the Saint. The man beside the bag-pipe player has a peacock feather in his hat, which is symbol of pride.

Years later, people rediscovered the peasant paintings. They did not know very much about the artist and decided that Bruegel must have been a talented peasant. He was nicknamed 'Peasant Bruegel'.

Later still, people realised that Bruegel's paintings were done by an extraordinarily talented artist. Since 1900 his work has become very popular and it has been carefully studied. Now we understand more about what Bruegel was trying to show us through his paintings.

Marriage to Mayken

Pieter Bruegel married Mayken Coeck van Aelst in Brussels in 1563. Mayken was the daughter of Pieter Coeck, Bruegel's old teacher. Pieter Coeck had studios in both Brussels and Antwerp, but died in 1550 long before the marriage.

Pieter and Mayken lived together in Brussels for six years and had two sons: Pieter who was born in 1564 and Jan, born in 1568. In September 1569, Pieter Bruegel died and was buried in Notre Dame de la Chapelle in Brussels. He was probably only 44 years old.

Mayken lived on for another nine years raising her young sons, who could barely have known their father. She may have returned to Antwerp to live with relatives. Pieter was only 14 when she died and Jan could not have been more than 10.

Sadly, Bruegel left no letters or writings about his work and none of his friends wrote down conversations they may have had with Bruegel. So we have nothing but Bruegel's paintings to help us understand the message he was trying to give to the world.

◀ **Brussels, artist unknown**
In the 1500s Brussels was the capital of Brabant, one of the areas of the Low Lands. This painting, by an unknown Flemish artist, shows how Brussels would have looked when Bruegel lived there.

▲ **The Magpie on the Gallows, 1568**
Bruegel painted this the year before he died and left it to Mayken in his will. It is the lightest and brightest of landscapes, although at its centre is the place where people were hanged. Peasants dance merrily on the left of the painting and a magpie perches on top of the gallows. Experts have puzzled over the picture's meaning. Bruegel could be showing how death comes to all living things, even when life is good.

Thirty of the 48 paintings that still exist were painted during the last six years of Bruegel's life, which were spent in Brussels. With their sharp outlines and rich colours, the paintings are still full of life and energy. Today more people know his work than ever before and everyone now sees Bruegel's works as masterpieces.

The Brueghel family

Both of Bruegel's sons, Pieter and Jan, became painters and changed the spelling of their name back to Brueghel. Pieter Brueghel became a Master of the Guild at Antwerp in 1585 and is best known for his copies and variations of his father's peasant paintings. Other work showing hell-fire and demons earned him the nickname 'Hell Brueghel'.

Of the two sons, Jan was the more talented. He travelled to Cologne and Italy and became Dean of the Guild at Antwerp. He often visited Brussels and was a friend of Paul Rubens. He earned the name 'Velvet Brueghel'.

▼ Summer, Pieter Brueghel the Younger, about 1620
Pieter Brueghel painted many versions of his father's prints and paintings of rural scenes.

▶ **Vase of Flowers, Jan Brueghel, 1607–08**
If you look closely at this vase of roses and tulips, you can see insects crawling over the leaves and different stages in the life-cycle of a moth lying on the table by the vase.

■ *Jan Brueghel painted many versions of the same subject. There are slight differences between them – always to do with the objects shown on the table. Because there was such a great demand for his flower pictures, Jan Brueghel knew he could repeat certain paintings and still be sure of selling them.*

This was due to his skill in creating delicate textures, like those you can see in this flower painting. He was considered the best flower painter of his day and his paintings were much sought after.

Sons and grandsons followed in the Brueghel family tradition, but the talent dwindled and disappeared as the generations went on. None of the descendants ever matched the talent of Pieter the Elder and Younger or Jan.

More information

Glossary

amphitheatre A building that is round or oval in shape, with seats rising in layers around its sides and a space in the centre where things happen.

canvas Woven cloth on which artists paint in oils. The cloth must first be sealed with a coating known as a ground and stretched on a frame.

guild A group of people with the same interests or who do the same kind of work, such as craftsmen or merchants, who meet regularly to help each other.

humanism In the Middle Ages in Europe, the Church was thought to be more important than individual people. Writers such as Erasmus began to change this point of view, saying that human beings should be put first.

landscape A painting in which scenery is the main subject of a picture.

merchant A person who buys and sells goods, often trading with other countries.

Middle Ages The time in history from about AD1000 to 1400.

moral A lesson we are taught about how people should behave, often through a story.

mythology Collections of stories which have been told and retold. They are sometimes about gods and goddesses, and often try to explain things about the world. Different countries have their own myths.

parable A story with a message about how people should behave. There are many parables told by Jesus in the New Testament.

patron A person who takes a special interest in an artist, paying the artist to paint pictures or collecting his or her work.

peasant A worker who farms land owned by a landowner. Peasant men and women in the Middle Ages led very hard lives, often working long hours in the fields.

proverb A short saying containing a wise message or fact.

self-portrait A painting an artist does of him or herself, often by looking in a mirror.

People

Hieronymus Bosch (about 1450–1516) A Flemish artist, famous for his strange and nightmarish paintings.

Jan van Eyck (1390–1441) This Flemish artist was one of the earliest painters in oil. He developed the technique to a high quality.

Johann Gutenberg (about 1396-1468) Invented a printing press with movable type. Books could now be printed quickly and easily.

Titian (about 1487–1576) A great painter from the Italian city of Venice, particularly known for his rich use of colour in portraits, religious paintings and scenes from mythology. The name Titian is short Tiziano Vecelli.

Michelangelo (1475–1564) Great Italian artist who was especially interested in the human form. His magnificent sculptures and a massive series of paintings on the ceiling of the Sistine chapel in Rome are his masterpieces.

Peter Paul Rubens (1577-1640) A successful Flemish artist. He studied in Rome and, on his return to Antwerp, produced many splendid paintings, filled with colour, movement and light.

Index

Page numbers in **bold** *show that there is a picture on that page.*

Acknowledgments

This book wouldn't be possible without the collaboration of Chris Thomas, Martin Amor and James Smith, and the help of the Kickstarter community and all the backers who made this project a reality, especially Zan Boag, Joanna Hoyle, Andrew Walsh, Thomas Gier, Matt Haworth, Ralph Caspers, Katryne Gélineau, Edgar Gallart, Bonfire Creative Intelligence and Ruth Ann Harnisch.

Syncretism.

The attempt to reconcile disparate, even contradictory, beliefs into one belief structure.

Symbolism.

The practice of using something (such as an image, symbol or word) to mean something other than itself.

Pacifism.

In ethics or politics, an opposition to war or violence. This ranges from advocacy of peaceful solutions to problems, to a stance where all violence or force is considered morally wrong.

Legalism.

The strict adherence to a legislative text, such as a constitution, federal law or religious scripture.

Nominalism.

The belief that universal or mental concepts have no objective reality, and exist only as the words or "names" we give them.

Dynamism.

The idea that the material world can be understood as active forces, the movement and interaction of which form the basis of all phenomena in the universe.

Structuralism.

The theory that individual phenomena cannot be understood except through understanding the wider structure, or context, of their interrelations.

Epiphenomenalism.

The view that physical events have effects on mental processes, but that mental processes have no physical effects whatsoever.

Emotivism.

The assertion that all individual ethical judgements are purely expressions of one's own attitude intended to change the actions or attitudes of others.

Eternalism.

The philosophical position that time is just another dimension, that future events already exist, and that all points in time are equally real.

Finalism.

The assertion that any event is defined by a pre-set final outcome, and that all events leading up to that outcome are shaped by it.

Dialetheism.

The view that some statements can be true and false at the same time, known as a "true contradiction".

Perspectivism.

Philosophical view that all ideas come from different perspectives and are caused by specific inner drives, and that any ethical judgement can be made from any number of viewpoints.

Spiritualism.

The belief that spirits of the dead can be contacted through certain mediums, and that the guidance of the dead can be of spiritual value.

Reconstructivism.

A philosophy that holds that societies should continually reform in order to establish a more perfect government or social network.

Utopia.

The many various social and political movements based upon the idea that paradise is achievable on earth.

Subjectivism.

The view that one's own mind is the only unquestionable proof of existence, and that subjective experience is the root of all meaning in the world.

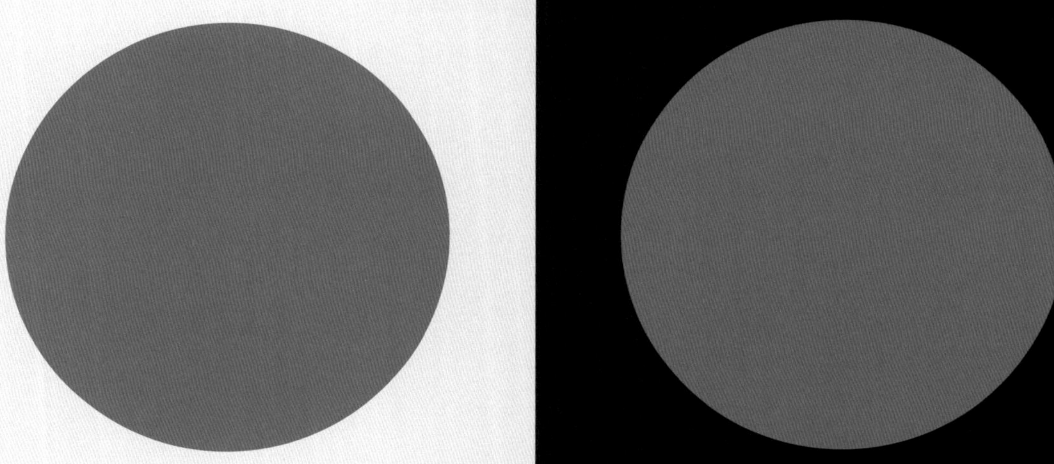

Instrumentalism.

The idea that the truth of knowledge is irrelevant, and that knowledge should be judged by its usefulness.

Pragmatism.

The view that practicality and utility should be vital components of meaning and truth, rather than basing actions on abstract or intellectual concepts.

Innatism.

The belief that the mind is born with ideas and knowledge, rather than learning it as you go through life.

Positivism.

The position that the only authentic knowledge is that acquired through scientific means.

Atomism.

The theory that all things in the universe are composed of very small, indestructible elements.

Hy

The philosophica

Naturalism.

A range of philosophical stances that do not distinguish the supernatural from nature, and thus claim that they can be studied using the same methods.

Illusionism.

A philosophy that holds that there is no material world but rather a collection of illusions formed by human consciousness that results in an environment that all humans live within.

Phenomenalism.

The view that physical things do not exist as things in themselves, but as a set of sensory stimuli that we experience or perceive.

Realism.

The belief that reality exists independently of our own observation or perception.

Externalism.

The position that the mind and human experience is not just the result of the nervous system and brain, but also the phenomena that exist outside of it.

Solipsism.

The view that only direct mental experience is certain, as things external to one's own mind cannot be known.

Contextualism.

A range of views that argue that a phenomenon can only be properly understood within the context it occurred.

Mysticism.

The pursuit of a state of consciousness or being that profoundly explains or transcends reality.

Meliorism.

The idea that humans can, through their interference with natural processes, produce a more desirable outcome than the natural one.

Objectivism.

In ethics, the belief that certain acts are objectively right or wrong.

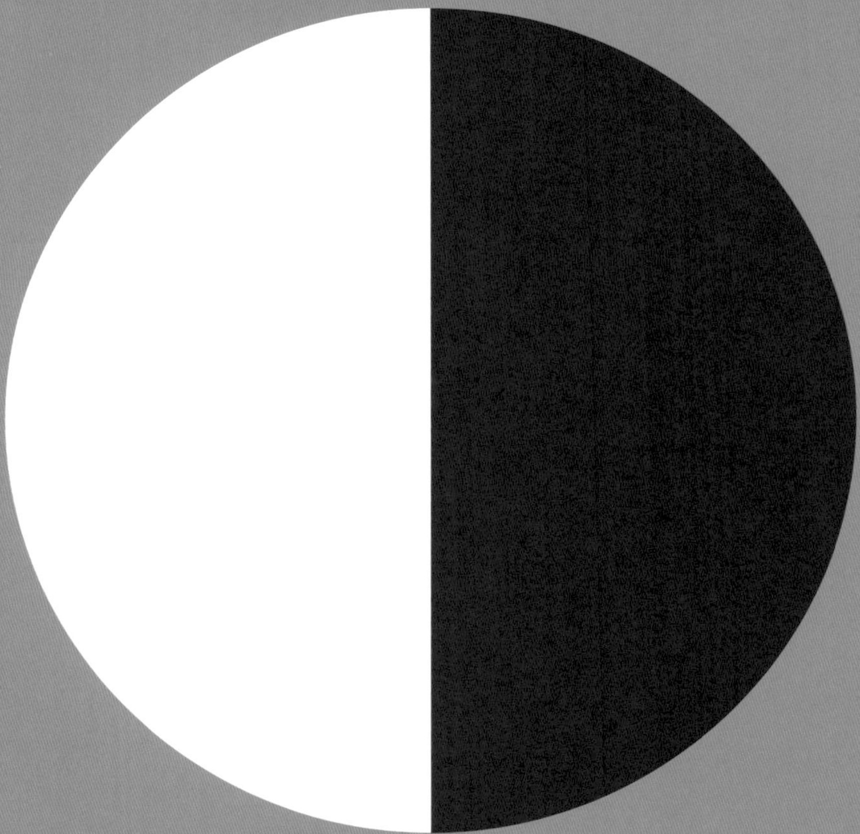

Universalism.

The belief that there are philosophical concepts that have universal application and relevance.

Deontologism.

An ethical system that judges the morality of an action according to its adherence a set of pre-defined principles, rather than, for example, its consequences.

Compatibilism.

The theory that free will and determinism are compatible - that choices in life could have been made differently had different circumstances preceded them.

Indeterminism.

The philosophical belief contradictory to determinism: that there are events that are in some way uncaused.

Occasionalism.

A theory denying efficient causation between mundane events, instead believing that all events are caused directly by a God or higher power.

Pantheism.

The view that nature and God are the same thing; that everything in the universe is of an all-encompassing God.

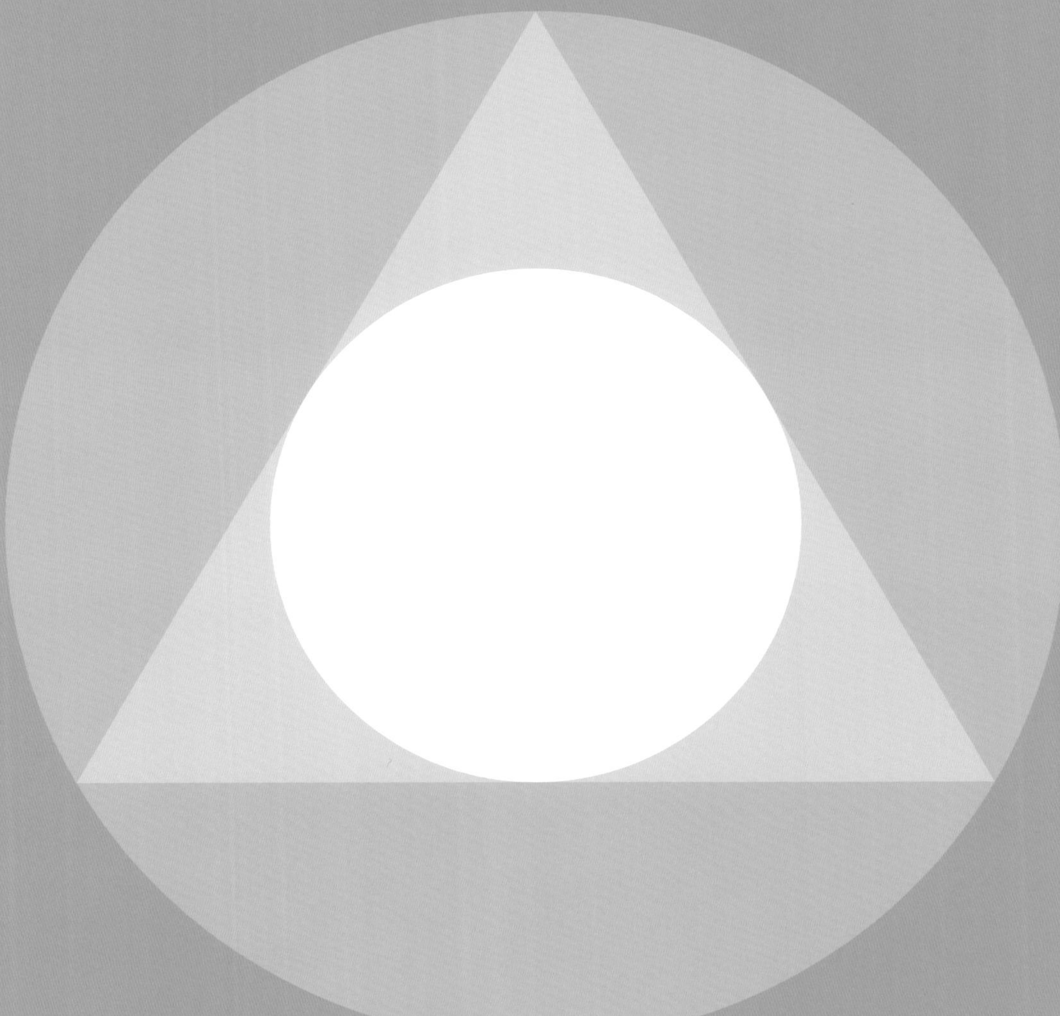

Consequentialism.

The view that the consequences of a potential action or policy are the most important considerations when debating whether or not to go ahead with it.

Utilitarianism.

The school of ethics that strives towards the maximisation of welfare for the maximum number of people.

Extropy.

A system of ethics concerned with negotiating the gradual improvement of the human condition that is occurring due to advances in technology.

Transhumanism.

A movement supporting the use of new technology to enhance human potential and eliminate undesirable aspects of the human condition, such as suffering, disease and ageing.

Cynicism.

The lack of belief in selfless or sincere human qualities, such as altruism, honesty or virtue, believing instead that people are driven only by self-interest.

Ethnocentrism.

The tendency to view the world with one's own culture and identity at the center of everything.

Feminism.

A range of social and moral philosophies concerned with the experiences of women in society, most often with the intent of eradicating gender inequality.

Egalitarianism.

A political ideology that holds that all people should be treated as equals.

Pluralism.

The position that there are many contrasting principles, essences and substances forming the basis of all phenomena.

Secularism.

The idea that bodies of government should be completely separate from religious institutions.

Totalitarianism.

A political ideology in which a state enforces national loyalty and identity in order to mobilise or oppress its population.

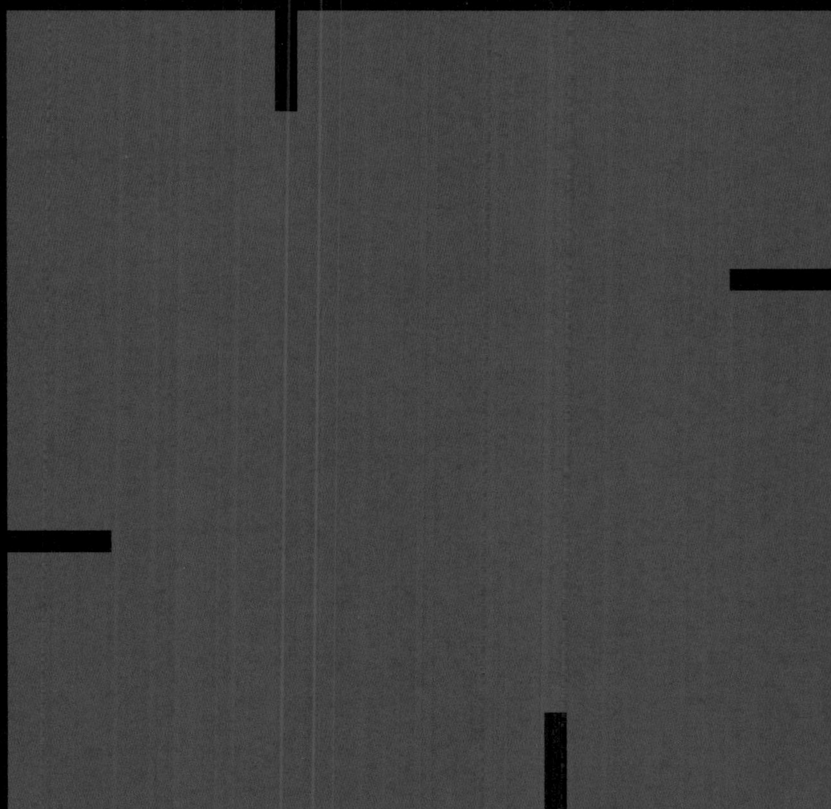

Socialism.

An economic system in which the means of production are owned and controlled by the many rather than the few.

Anarchism.

A range of views that oppose the idea of the state as a means of governance, instead advocating a society based on non-hierarchical relationships.

Authoritarianism.

The organization of society through strong, often oppressive measures against its people.

Collectivism.

A view that places emphasis on the group over the individual, often holding the belief that the “greater good” of the group is more important than the good of any individual within it.

Individualism.

The political stance that the rights of individuals should be protected over that of collectives, such as states, religions or social groups.

Anthropocentrism.

The conviction that the existence of human beings is the central reason for the universe's existence.

Humanism.

A range of ethical views that consider human nature to be the source of morality.

Capitalism.

An economic system based on the production of goods for profit, and the private ownership of the means of production.

Historicism.

The theory that to understand a historical event, you must understand the philosophical context that it took place in, rather than explain it with supposedly timeless or fundamental ideas.

Monism.

The metaphysical and theological view that there is only one principle, essence, substance or energy that forms the basis of all phenomena.

Dualism.

The conviction that all concepts within the world fundamentally consist of two contrasting qualities, such as good and evil, or body and mind.

Formalism.

The view that in any cultural product, it is the form rather than the content that provides true meaning.

Aestheticism.

The belief that our main efforts in life should be focused on creating and enjoying beauty, in all its forms.

Materialism.

The philosophical view that the only thing that can truly be said to 'exist' is matter; that fundamentally, all things are composed of 'material' and all phenomena are the result of material interactions.

Idealism.

The philosophical view that asserts that reality is fundamentally based on, and shaped by, ideas and mental experience, rather than material forces.

Mechanicism.

The theory that all natural phenomena can be explained by physical causes, that they can be understood through their parts and functions rather than any holistic interpretation.

Vitalism.

The doctrine that "vital forces", often equated with the soul, are active in living organisms, and that life cannot be explained solely by material or mechanism.

Egoism.

The ethical position that conscious beings ought to always do what is in their own self-interest.

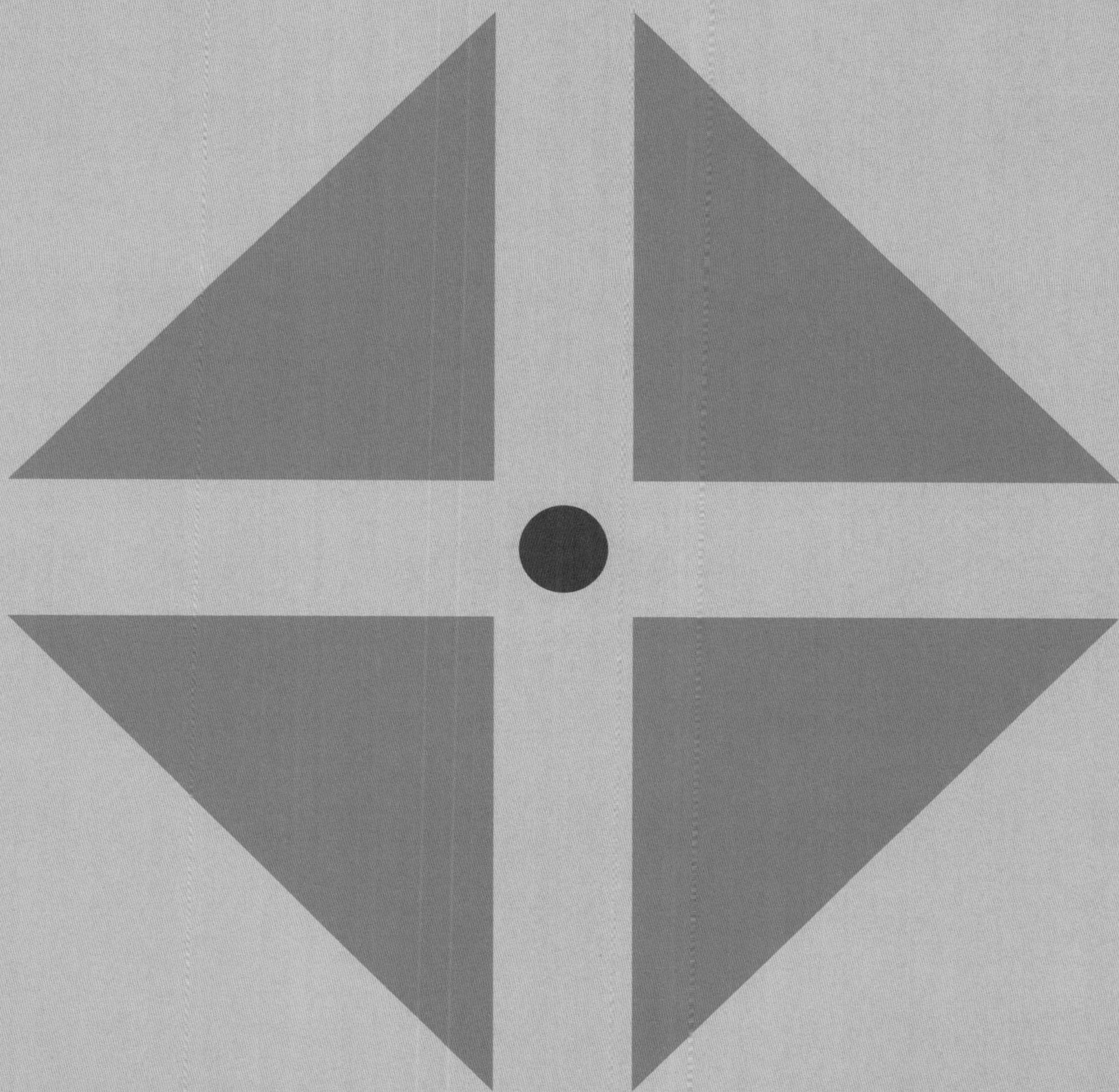

Altruism.

The practice and principle of using actions to benefit others, expecting nothing in return.

Eudaimonism.

A system of ethics that evaluates actions in terms of their capacity to produce happiness.

Stoicism.

The principle that emotional and physical self-control leads to inner peace and strength, allowing one to live a happier life.

Asceticism.

An approach to life typified by restraining from worldly pleasures, in order to pursue a more virtuous or enlightened existence.

Hedonism.

The ethical position that pleasure is the ultimate goal and greatest good, and should be the central aim of all decisions made.

Inductionism.

The view that scientific progress is guided by the various observations made in previous experiments, and that statements of truth should be based on this mass of observations.

Deductionism.

A view of how scientific knowledge should be acquired - by first proposing a hypothesis, then attempting to prove it wrong through empirical tests on observable data.

Deconstructivism.

A school of thought dedicated to critiquing the assumptions and ideas that form the basis of our understanding of the world.

Constructivism.

The view that reality, and the methods we use to understand it, are man-made, subjective constructions rather than an objective reading of events.

Absurdism.

The contention that the attempts of man to find meaning in the universe will ultimately fail because no such meaning exists.

Skepticism.

The method of practicing doubt when regarding what is held as knowledge.

Existentialism.

The idea that all philosophical thought must begin with the experiences of the individual, and it is up to the individual to give meaning and authenticity to their own existence.

Nihilism.

The philosophical view that the world,
purpose, truth, or value.

Atheism.

The absence of belief that gods or deities exist.

Theism.

The belief that a god or deity is present and active in the universe.

Eclecticism.

A conceptual approach that does not stick to a single paradigm or set of assumptions, but instead draws upon multiple theories or styles to gain a more varied or balanced insight into something.

Dogma.

The inflexible adherence to a rigid doctrine or ideology, not open to rational argument or debate.

Rationalism.

The theory that human reason can be the source of all knowledge.

Empiricism.

The scientific doctrine stating that all knowledge ultimately comes from sensory experience and observable evidence, rather than intuition or pre-conceived ideas.

Pessimism.

A state of mind in which one believes only the worst to be possible; the philosophical view that the world is as bad as can be.

Optimism.

Historically, the philosophical position that this is the best of all possible worlds, more often used to describe a cheerful or positive worldview.

Reductionism.

The idea that the nature of complex things can always be reduced and explained by simpler, more fundamental truths.

Holism.

The theory that the properties of a system cannot be understood by the sum of its parts alone, but by how the system behaves as a whole.

Relativism.

The assertion that no belief can be said to have absolute truth, having value only within a certain context or frame of reference.

Absolutism.

The position that within a particular school of thought, all different perspectives are either absolutely true or absolutely false.

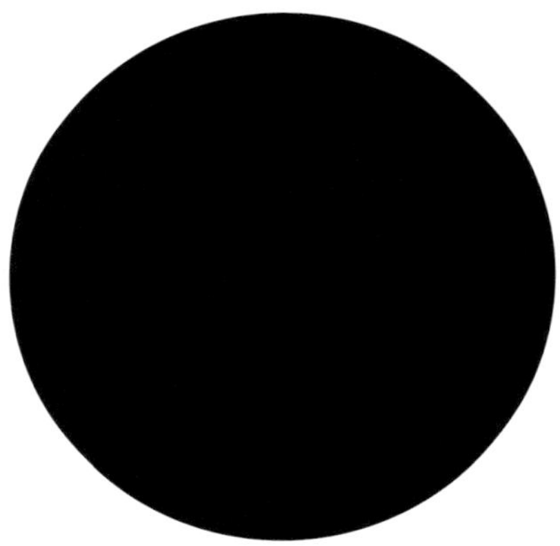

Free will.

The ability of conscious agents to be free to make their own decisions, free of any social, moral or political constraints.

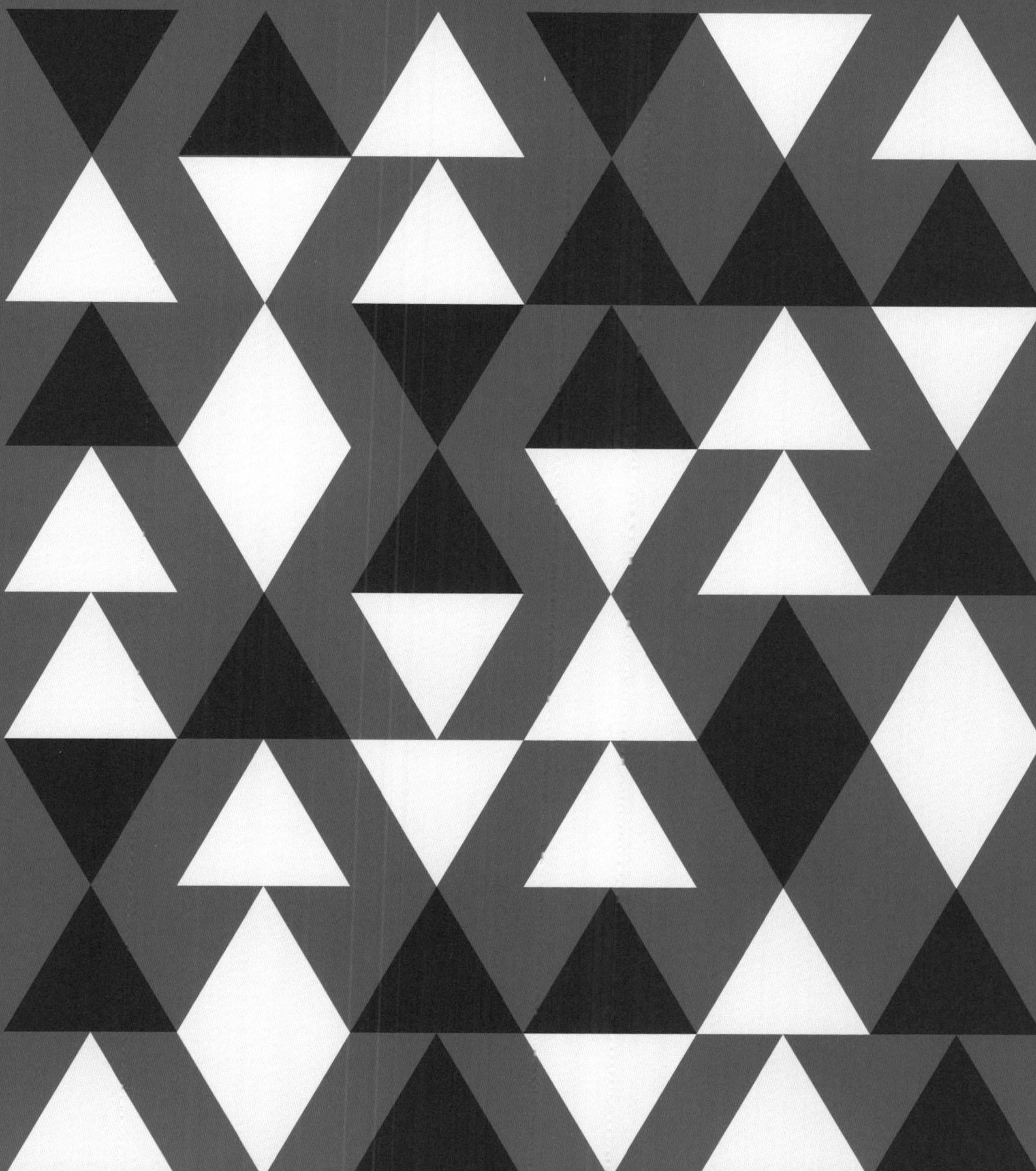

Determinism.

The proposition that all events, including those of human thoughts, are causally determined by an unbroken chain of prior events.

Philographics.

Genís Carreras

Philographics:
Big ideas in simple shapes

Published by Genis Carreras
First edition — May 2013
Created and designed by Genis Carreras
Text by Chris Thomas

ISBN
978-0-9576786-0-6

www.geniscarreras.com
Twitter: @gex00